What's for lunch?

Honey

D1383311

Library of Congress Cataloging-in-Publication Data
Robson, Pam.
    Honey / written by Pam Robson. --1st American ed.
    p.   cm. -- (What's for Lunch?)
    Includes index.
    Summary: Explains how bees produce honey, as well as the
    commercial process of producing and marketing honey as a food
    and for use in other products.
    ISBN 0-516-20825-X
    1. Bee culture--Juvenile literature. 2. Honey--Juvenile
literature. [1. Bee culture. 2. Honey] I. Title. II. Series:
Robson, Pam. What's for Lunch?
SF523.5.R63 1998   97.6503
638'.1--dc21   CIP
                                                AC

© 1997 Franklin Watts
96 Leonard Street
London
EC2A 4RH

First American edition 1998 by
Franklin Watts
A Division of Grolier Publishing
Sherman Turnpike
Danbury, CT 06816

ISBN 0-516-20825-X (lib. bdg.)
ISBN 0-516-26220-3 (pbk)

Editor: Samantha Armstrong
Designer: Kirstie Billingham
Consultant: Godfrey Munro, Park Bee Keeping Supplies
Reading Consultant: Prue Goodwin, Reading and Language
Information Centre, Reading.

Printed in Hong Kong

What's for lunch?

Honey

Pam Robson

CHILDREN'S PRESS®

A Division of Grolier Publishing

LONDON • NEW YORK • HONG KONG • SYDNEY
DANBURY, CONNECTICUT

J
X
638.1
Rob

NORTH BAY PUBLIC LIBRARY
SEP 1999
DISCARDED

A 4-8

Today we are having honey for lunch.
Honey is a sweet, sticky food.
Lots of people spread honey on their bread.
Eating honey gives you **energy**.
Honey also contains **vitamins** and
minerals to keep you healthy.

Honey is made by bees.

Bees are **insects** with six legs and four wings.

They make honey and wax,

and **pollinate** our plants and trees.

They make honey from **nectar,**

which they collect from flowers.

They eat the honey in winter when there are

no flowers to collect nectar from.

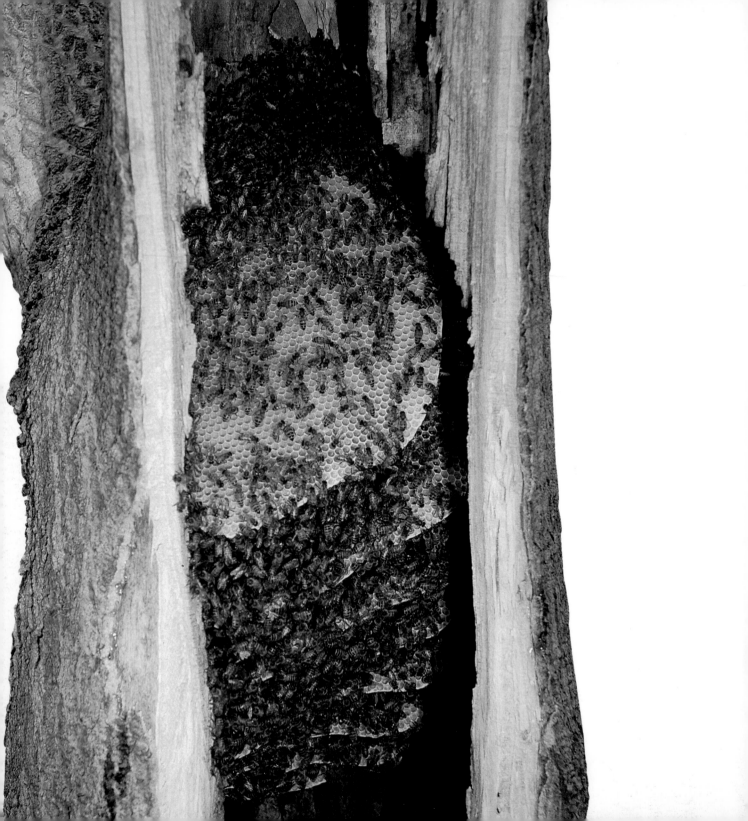

People have always collected honey
from bees in the wild.
Wild bees live in holes in trees
or in gaps under rocks.
Most bees, however, are kept in **hives**
so that people can collect the honey easily.

People who keep bees are called **apiarists**.
They wear special hats and gloves
to protect them against bee stings.
Inside the hives are upright wooden frames.
The bees make wax in their stomachs.
They use the wax to make a **honeycomb**
on each frame.
The honeycomb has hundreds of
six-sided compartments called **cells**.

Every hive has a **queen bee**.
She eats a special, rich food
called **royal jelly,**
which makes her large.
Male bees are called **drones**.
They **fertilize** the queen.
The queen lays lots of eggs.
Each egg is laid in one of the cells
in the honeycomb.

Female bees are called **workers**.
They collect nectar from flowers.
They may fly many miles to find it.
When they return, they perform a dance
to show the others where the nectar
can be found.

The honey is **filtered**
and left to stand until
all the bubbles of air
have disappeared.
Now the honey is ready.
Most honey we buy
is a blend of
different kinds of honey.
They are mixed together
in a factory and
then put into jars
or other containers.

A label is put onto every jar
to tell people what kind of honey it is.

The jars of honey are put into boxes
and taken by truck and boat all over the world.
They are sold in shops and supermarkets.

Honey comes in different colors.
The color and taste of honey
depend on the nectar
collected by the bees.

Some honey is dark brown and
some is light yellow.
Honey made by wild bees in Zambia
tastes different from Mexican honey.

Honey was once used
instead of sugar to sweeten food.
It is still used today to sweeten drinks.
It is very soothing to add honey
to a lemon drink when your throat is sore.
You can use honey
to bake a Russian honey cake.

Honey has other uses too.
It can be used in soap
to make your skin soft.
The wax that the bees produce
for the honeycomb can be used
to make candles.
Look how many things we get from bees!

Glossary

apiarist   a person who keeps bees

blend   to mix different substances together

cells   the six-sided compartments of a honeycomb

drone bee   a male bee that stays in the hive to mate
                    with, or fertilize, the queen bee

energy   the strength to work and play

fertilize   to create new life; the drone bee fertilizes
                    the queen. Then the queen bee lays eggs.

filtered   the honey is passed through a mesh or filter to
                    clean it and remove any bits of honeycomb

hive   a wooden structure in which bees live

honeycomb   a wax layer of six-sided cells made by bees.
                    Honey is stored in the honeycomb, and
                    the queen bee lays her eggs there.

honey sac   a special bag inside the stomach of a bee
                    in which nectar is stored

30

insect	an animal with three pairs of legs, three parts to its body, and usually wings
mineral	something found in honey that helps to build strong bones and muscles
nectar	a sugary liquid made by flowers
pollinate	to carry pollen from one flower to another
queen bee	a large female bee. She is the leader in the hive and the only bee that lays eggs.
royal jelly	food fed by worker bees to a queen bee to help her grow large
vitamin	something found in honey and fresh fruit and vegetables that helps us stay healthy
worker bee	a female bee whose job is to collect nectar from flowers

NORTH BAY PUBLIC LIBRARY SEP 1 - 1999

Index

Picture credits: FLPA 6 (T. Davidson), 8 (S. Maslowski), 9 (David Grewcock), 14 (Silvestris), 15 (T. Davidson), 19 (P. Moulu/Sunset); Holt Studios 7 (Nigel Cattlin), 11 (Nigel Cattlin), 12-13 (Nigel Cattlin); NHPA 16 (Stephen Dalton); By kind permission of Rowse Honey, Wallingford, England 20-21 (Steve Shott), 22 (Steve Shott), 23(Steve Shott); Nick Bailey Photography cover, 3, 5. All other photographs Tim Ridley, Wells Street Studio, London. **With thanks to Edward Evans and Jessica Hopf.**